Trace Taylor

Chocolate

This is chocolate.

We love chocolate in brownies.

We love chocolate in cake.

We love chocolate in milk.

This is a tree.

There is fruit on the tree.

There are seeds in the fruit.

The chocolate comes from these seeds.

Chocolate

We take the fruit.

We get the seeds.

We take the seeds here.

We make this with them.

Then we make this.

We make ice cream with it.

We put it in milk.

We make chocolate chips.

We put them in cookies.

We make pies.

We make many things with chocolate.

We love chocolate.

Where Chocolate Grows

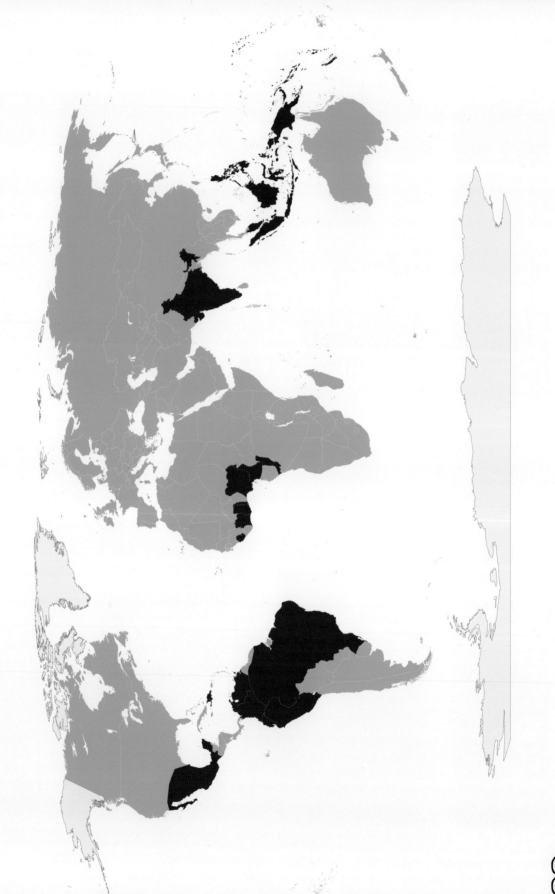

Practice With National Reading Standards

1. Tell 3 things that you learned about chocolate. (CCSS 2)

2. Using the words *first*, *second*, and *third*, explain how chocolate is made. Use the pictures to help you tell the story. (CCSS 3)

For more information about the National Reading Standards, please visit
www.americanreadingathome.com/common-core-standards

Power Words

How many can you read?

	this	we	with	
take	the	them	then	there
it	love	make	on	put
from	get	here	in	is
a	are	come		